Holly Days

Celebrating Christmas with Rhymes, Songs, Art Projects, Games, and Snacks

By SUSAN OLSON HIGGINS
Illustrated by MARION HOPPING EKBERG

Totline® Publications
A Division of Frank Schaffer Publications
Torrance, California

Thank you to my special sons, friends, relatives, and those who have given their support and shared the love and joyful spirit of this holiday through the years. God bless you!

A special thank you to those talented and lovely people who assisted in putting this collection together.

—Susan Olson Higgins

Totline Publications would like to thank the following people for their contributions to this book: Donna Mullennix, Thousand Oaks, CA.

Managing Editor: Kathleen Cubley
Editor: Elizabeth McKinnon
Contributing Editors: Gayle Bittinger, Carol Gnojewski, Susan Hodges, Susan Sexton, Jean Warren
Copyeditor: Kris Fulsaas
Proofreader: Miriam Bulmer
Editorial Assistant: Durby Peterson
Graphic Designer (Interior): Sarah Ness
Layout Artist: Gordon Frazier
Graphic Designer (Cover): Brenda Mann Harrison
Production Manager: Melody Olney

ISBN: 1-57029-267-1

Printed in the United States of America
Published by Totline® Publications
Editorial Office: P.O. Box 2250
    Everett, WA 98203
Business Office: 23740 Hawthorne Blvd.
    Torrance, CA 90505

Contents

Celebrating Christmas

The celebration of Christmas has come to mean many different things to different people. Traditions have been developed and passed on from generation to generation until there is now a wealth of customs surrounding the holiday.

In the United States, the joy of Christmas comes wrapped in shining lights, jolly Santas, carol singing, cookies baking, kisses under mistletoe, glimmering trees, the warmth of family, and brightly colored packages. And underlying the festivities, the true meaning of Christmas speaks to minds and hearts through the spirit of giving.

The Christmas Tree

It is believed that the Christmas tree custom originated in Germany. In olden times, it was common practice to welcome guests by lighting candles on a tree. Eventually, the delightful practice evolved into a Christmas tradition that today uses colorful lights in place of candles.

Christmas Cards

This custom began in England when beautiful greetings were hand-painted onto cards in designs of flowers, birds, and so forth. Gradually the popularity of sending Christmas cards grew until it became one of the most delightful traditions of the season, bringing old friends and family close to heart at holiday time.

Saint Nicholas

Saint Nicholas lived in the fourth century and devoted his life to helping others, especially children. Today, in many countries, Saint Nicholas's Day is celebrated on December 6, when children look forward to receiving gifts.

Saint Nicholas has different names in different lands, such as Father Christmas in England and Le Père Nöel in France. In America, he is known as Santa Claus, the jolly old man in a red suit with his team of reindeer and a sleigh.

No matter what Saint Nicholas is called or when he arrives, everywhere he goes he delivers gifts and the spirit of love and joy to children.

Christmas Stockings

Legend has it that long ago Santa was flying over housetops in his sleigh when he dropped some coins down a chimney, intending them to land on the hearth. Instead, the coins fell into some stockings that were hanging by the fire to dry. It is said that from then on, stockings have been hung by the chimney in hopes that Santa will fill them to the brim!

Other Ways to Say "Merry Christmas!"

Spanish—Feliz Navidad
(fay-LEES nah-vee-DOD)

German—Fröhliche Weihnachten
(FREW-lick-uh VYE-nock-ten))

French—Joyeux Nöel
(zhwah-YOU no-ELL)

Italian—Buon Natale
(bwan nah-TALL-eh)

Swedish—God Jul
(goo-d YOOL)

A Word About Safety—All of the activities in this book are appropriate for children ages 4 to 6. However, it is important that an adult supervise the activities to make sure that children do not put any materials or objects in their mouth. As for art materials, such as scissors, glue, or felt tip markers, use those that are specifically labeled as safe for children unless the materials are to be used only by an adult.

Rhymes & Songs

Busy Elves

One little elf sat on Santa's knee.

Two little elves trimmed the Christmas tree.

Three little elves shined the reindeer hoofs.

Four little elves counted children's roofs.

Five little elves painted all the trains.

Six little elves wrapped candy canes.

Seven little elves bounced Christmas balls.

Eight little elves dressed pretty dolls.

Nine little elves put toys in the sleigh,

Getting all ready for Christmas day.

Susan Olson Higgins

Peeking

There are his toes!
There's his foot!
There's an ankle
Covered with soot!

There's his leg!
I see his knee!
This is it!
He's visiting me!

I see his waist
And big black belt.
I see his shirt
Of bright red felt!

There's his arm!
What's in his hand?
I think this year
Will be just grand!

There's a shoulder!
Look, his head!
I'm so glad
I'm not in bed!

What's he doing?
I can't see.
He's over by
The Christmas tree.

He's near the stockings
Where they're hung.
He is turning—
Oh, he must be done.

Back to the chimney,
Up he goes.
He's disappeared
From head to toes.

Now I know.
It's true, you see—
Santa's as real
As real can be!
Susan Olson Higgins

Santa's Spy

I just saw him!
Didn't you?
One of Santa's elves
Just peeked through!

He pressed his nose
On the windowpane.
His hat was covered
With candy canes.

I think he's here
To see if I'm good,
And doing all
The things I should.

I'm sure I saw him
Peeking in right there!
I think I'll be good now—
"Would you like to share?"
Susan Olson Higgins

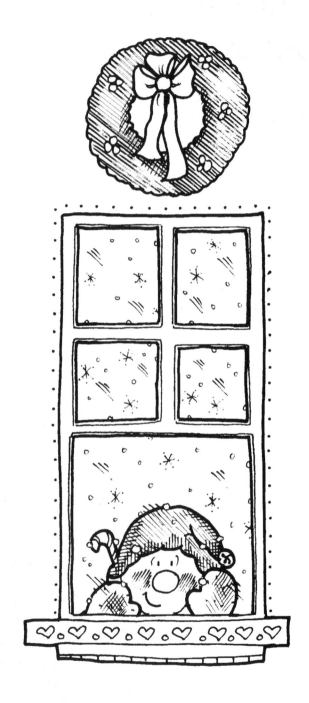

Waiting for Christmas

When will Christmas ever be here?
I think I'm going to explode!
Do you think Santa packed enough?
Can the reindeer carry the load?

When will Christmas ever be here?
I can hardly wait!
I try to be patient—but I can't!
Why is Christmas so late?

When will Christmas ever be here?
The days go by sooo slow!
I've been waiting and waiting so long—
Oh! Now where did Christmas go?

Susan Olson Higgins

Santa
Action Rhyme

Blink, blink,

Turn around,

Santa's on his way.

Jump, jump,

Clap your hands,

Hop into his sleigh.

Down, up,

Up, down,

Bending, oh, so slow.

Cross your arms,

Touch your head,

Up the chimney you go!

As you recite the rhyme, encourage your child
to act out the movements described.

Susan Olson Higgins

Christmas Clapping

Come and clap this poem with me.

Clap your hands or clap your knee.

Clap two for yes or three for no.

Clap the answers as we go.

Let's begin—

Santa Claus is a big mouse.
  (Clap, clap, clap)

Elves live in a mushroom house.
  (Clap, clap, clap)

Christmas trees are always blue.
  (Clap, clap, clap)

I can jump a mountain, can you?
  (Clap, clap, clap)

Santa Claus is dressed in red.
  (Clap, clap)

He won't come till you're in bed.
  (Clap, clap)

Reindeer pull old Santa's sleigh.
  (Clap, clap)

He leaves toys for Christmas day.
  (Clap, clap)

Santa Claus has two green ears.
  (Clap, clap, clap)

He's been asleep for years and years.
  (Clap, clap, clap)

Santa Claus walks on his hands.
  (Clap, clap, clap)

He grows taller whenever he stands.
  (Clap, clap, clap)

Santa's sleigh flies underground.
  (Clap, clap, clap)

Reindeer make a roaring sound.
  (Clap, clap, clap)

Now my silly poem is through.
  (Clap, clap)

Write more verses, please, will you?
  (Clap, clap)

Susan Olson Higgins

The Elf Clown

Stand in a circle,

Hold hands tight.

Begin to walk

To the right.

Now everybody

Spin around.

Slap your knee,

Then touch the ground.

Jump up tall,

Tap your toe.

Tap it fast,

Tap it slow.

Snap your fingers,

Reach up high.

Clap your hands

High in the sky.

All you elves

Sit right down.

Choose someone

To be Elf Clown.

Recite the rhyme for your child and his friends, and have everyone act out the movements. Then help choose someone to be the Elf Clown and lead the group in a game of Follow the Leader. Continue until everyone has had a turn.

Susan Olson Higgins

The Magical Trip

The reindeer leaped over a laughing brook—
They wanted to take another look
To see if Santa was ready to go
Over candy mountains and ice cream snow.

Santa nodded. It was time
To take their magical Christmas climb.
So up over rooftops they did glide,
Finally taking their Christmas ride.

They stopped up on each chocolate house,
Greeted by a sugar plum mouse,
While Santa delivered each magical toy
To every gingerbread girl and boy.

Then up and over the silvery trees,
Past sleepy bears and bumblebees,
They sailed on till twilight came,
And then they flew back home again.

Susan Olson Higgins

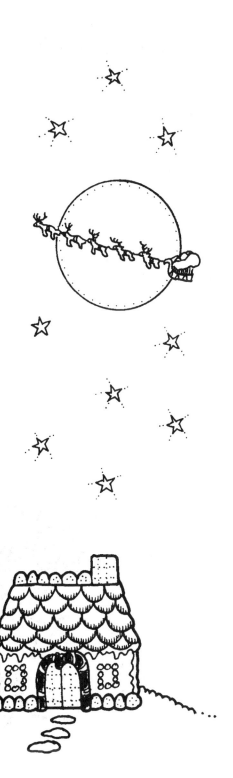

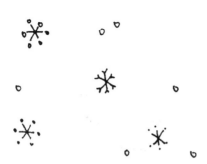

Snowy Christmas

Snow tumble-umbles downy-down,
Covering the branches and the ground.
Listen to the hush-hush quiet sound.
It looks like Christmas all around!
Susan Olson Higgins

The Family at Christmas

The family gathers
Around the tree,
Caroling, singing
On Christmas Eve.

Shoulder to shoulder,
Their hearts harmonize.
Together for Christmas,
They each realize

Their song of joy
That fills the air
Is their greatest gift—
The love they share.
Susan Olson Higgins

Around the Tree

Sung to: "The Farmer in the Dell"

All around the tree

Is our family

Singing with joy and love,

Singing happily.

Father sings along.

Hear him sing the song.

Merry Christmas, everyone!

Father sings along.

Mother sings along.

Hear her sing the song.

Merry Christmas, everyone!

Mother sings along.

Brother sings along.

Hear him sing the song.

Merry Christmas, everyone!

Brother sings along.

Sister sings along.

Hear her sing the song.

Merry Christmas, everyone!

Sister sings along.

Kitty sings along.

Hear him sing the song.

Merry Christmas, everyone!

Kitty sings along.
  (Mew.)

Puppy sings along.

Hear her sing the song.

Merry Christmas, everyone!

Puppy sings along.
  (Arf.)

We all sing along.

We all sing along.

Merry Christmas, everyone!

We all sing along.

Susan Olson Higgins

Little Snowman

I'm a little snowman
Short and fat,
With eyes, nose, smile,
And a top hat.
When it's Christmas Eve
What do I see?
Santa and his reindeer
Flying over me!

Susan Olson Higgins

Christmas Star

Sung to: "Twinkle, Twinkle, Little Star"

Twinkle, twinkle, Christmas star,
You are loveliest by far,
Up on top of our tree
For everyone to see.
Twinkle, twinkle, Christmas star,
You are loveliest by far.

Susan Olson Higgins

Just for Fun

Santa's Sleigh

You Will Need

cardboard carton
utility knife
red gift-wrap
tape
glue
cotton balls

1. Find a cardboard carton large enough for your child to sit in.

2. Place the carton on the floor, open one end up, and use a utility knife to cut off the flaps.

3. Cover the carton with red gift-wrap and secure the edges with tape to make a "Santa Sleigh."

4. Let your child decorate the sleigh by gluing a line of fluffed-out cotton balls around the top edge.

5. Allow the glue to dry.

6. Invite your child to climb aboard Santa's Sleigh and take a ride whenever she wishes.

   For More Fun: Trim the sides of the carton to resemble the sides of a sleigh. Then let your child help paint the carton red before adding the cotton balls.

Poem, Pen, and Song

You Will Need

crayons or markers
paper
"The Magical Trip" (page 15)
Christmas music
pen

1. Give your child crayons or markers and a piece of paper.

2. Read "The Magical Trip" (page 15) to him.

3. Put on some Christmas music, such as Tchaikovsky's *The Nutcracker* or a similar favorite.

4. As your child listens to the music, ask him to draw a picture of Santa's magical trip, rereading the poem to him, if necessary.

5. When he has finished, encourage him to tell you about his picture as you write on his paper what he dictates.

For More Fun: Ask your child to tell you where he would like to go if he could take a ride with Santa.

Santa Chimney Puppet

You Will Need

half-pint milk carton
scissors
glue
red paper
pen
large craft stick
red crayon
cotton

1. Find a clean half-pint milk carton.

2. Cut off the top of the carton and cut a slit in the bottom.

3. Glue red paper to the sides of the carton to make a "chimney."

4. For a Santa, help your child draw a face on one end of a large craft stick.

5. Give her a small triangle cut from red paper to glue above the face for Santa's hat.

6. Let her use a crayon to color Santa's "body" red.

7. Give her cotton to glue on for Santa's beard and hat trim.

8. Slide the bottom of the craft stick through the slit in the bottom of the carton.

9. Show your child how to move her Santa puppet up and down inside the chimney as you recite rhymes or sing songs.

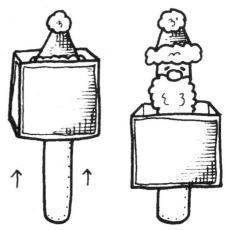

Snow Crystal Pictures

You Will Need

scissors
old Christmas cards
bowl
Epsom salts
boiling water
spoon
paintbrush

1. Cut the fronts off old Christmas cards.

2. In a bowl, mix equal amounts of Epsom salts and boiling water, stirring until the salts are dissolved.

3. Allow the mixture to cool.

4. Let your child use a clean paintbrush to cover the Christmas card fronts with the mixture.

5. As the mixture dries, crystals will appear, turning the pictures on the cards into sparkly Christmas scenes.

Toy Elf Hat

You Will Need

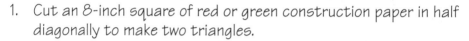

- scissors
- ruler
- red or green construction paper
- stapler
- glue
- collage materials
- teddy or other stuffed toy

1. Cut an 8-inch square of red or green construction paper in half diagonally to make two triangles.

2. Staple the two triangles together on the two short sides to make a hat.

3. Let your child decorate the hat by gluing on collage materials, such as Christmas gift-wrap scraps, holiday stickers, cotton balls, yarn pieces, ribbons and bows, or glitter.

4. When the glue has dried, have her put the Toy Elf Hat on the head of a teddy or other stuffed toy to dress it up for Christmas.

Christmas Snowflakes

You Will Need

fluted paper coffee filters
child-safe scissors
water
tape

1. Give your child a fluted paper coffee filter and a pair of child-safe scissors.

2. Show him how to flatten the filter with his hands and fold it into fourths, then eighths.

3. Help him cut triangles, half-circles, and other shapes out of the folded sides of the filter.

4. Have him open the filter to reveal a unique "snowflake."

5. Let him make as many snowflakes as he wishes.

6. Flatten the snowflakes completely by lightly dampening them with water, spreading them out on a tabletop, and allowing them to dry.

7. Tape the snowflakes to a windowpane for holiday decorations.

Stitch a Stocking

You Will Need

construction paper
scissors
hole punch
paint and paintbrush, crayons, or markers
yarn

1. Put together two sheets of construction paper and cut them into a large stocking shape.

2. Keeping the shapes together, use a hole punch to punch holes around the sides and bottom of the stocking as shown in the illustration.

3. Let your child decorate the shapes with paint, crayons, or markers.

4. Help her use a long piece of yarn to lace the two stocking shapes together, leaving the top open.

5. Tie on a loop of yarn and hang the stocking for a festive holiday decoration.

Christmas Banner

You Will Need

felt in various sizes and colors
scissors
glue
dowel or thin branch

1. Find a large square of felt (any color except green).

2. From green felt, cut out a simple Christmas tree shape to fit on the felt square.

3. Glue the tree in place.

4. Cut various colors of felt scraps into small pieces.

5. Invite your child to glue the pieces onto the tree for decorations.

6. Glue loops of felt to the top of the felt square for hangers.

7. When the glue has dried, insert a dowel or a thin branch through the hangers and display the banner as a holiday decoration.

3-D Christmas Tree

You Will Need

scissors
green construction paper
stapler or tape
Christmas stickers
glue
glitter

1. Cut a piece of green construction paper into a large half-circle.

2. Roll the half -circle into a cone shape and staple or tape it closed to make a "tree."

3. Invite your child to decorate the tree with Christmas stickers, glue, and glitter.

4. Stand the tree on a shelf or a table for a holiday decoration.

Macaroni Bell Ornament

You Will Need

scissors
thin cardboard
hole punch
glue
macaroni
gold spray paint
red yarn

1. Cut two bell shapes out of thin cardboard.

2. Using a hole punch, punch a hole at the top of each shape, making sure that the holes line up when the shapes are put together.

3. Let your child glue macaroni onto both bell shapes.

4. When the glue has dried, spray-paint the two shapes gold in an area away from your child.

5. Allow the paint to dry.

6. Glue the bell shapes together, back to back.

7. To complete the Macaroni Bell Ornament, tie on a loop of red yarn for a hanger.

   For More Fun: Make ornaments in other Christmas shapes, such as a wreath or a star.

Baked Clay Ornaments

You Will Need

bowl
measuring cup
flour
salt
water
rolling pin
ruler
Christmas cookie cutters
plastic straw
baking sheet
paintbrush
paint
glitter
yarn

1. In a bowl, combine 2 cups flour and 1 cup salt.

2. Pour in 2 cups water, a little at a time.

3. Knead for 7 to 10 minutes, adding a small amount of flour if the dough is too sticky or a small amount of water if it is too dry.

4. Using a rolling pin, roll out the dough to a ¼-inch thickness.

5. Let your child use cookie cutters to cut Christmas shapes out of the dough.

6. Poke a hole in the top of each shape with a plastic drinking straw.

7. Bake the shapes on a baking sheet in a 325°F oven for 30 minutes, or until hard.

8. When the shapes have cooled, let your child paint them with tempera paint and sprinkle on glitter.

9. Tie loops of yarn through the holes in the shapes for hanging.

Christmas Ornament Mobile

You Will Need

piece of driftwood or similar wood
screw eyes
scissors
fishing line
ornaments

1. Find a piece of driftwood or similar wood.

2. Insert a screw eye at each end of the piece of wood, as shown in the illustration.

3. Cut a long piece of fishing line and tie the ends to the screw eyes to make a hanger.

4. Insert several more screw eyes along the length of the wood, leaving spaces between them.

5. Ask your child to choose several Christmas ornaments that he has made (or let him make new ones for this project).

6. String the ornaments onto pieces of fishing line and tie them to the screw eyes in the wood piece to make a Christmas Ornament Mobile for hanging in your home.

Christmas Napkin Rings

You Will Need

scissors
paper towel tubes
ruler
glue
fabric, felt, or gift-wrap
stickers, yarn, or ribbon

1. Cut paper towel tubes into 2-inch-wide rings.

2. Help your child cover each ring by gluing on fabric, felt, or Christmas gift-wrap.

3. Let her decorate the rings with holiday stickers or glued-on pieces of yarn or ribbon.

4. Encourage her to give the napkin rings as early Christmas gifts to be used for the holidays.

Holiday Gift Towel

You Will Need

    white cotton dishtowel
    cardboard
    tape
    nontoxic fabric markers

1. Find a plain white cotton dishtowel.

2. Stretch the towel out on a piece of clean cardboard and tape the edges in place.

3. Let your child use nontoxic fabric markers to decorate the towel.

4. Encourage him to give the towel to someone special as a Christmas gift.

   Hint: Make sure your child wears protective clothing when working with fabric markers.

Painted Stone Paperweight

You Will Need

smooth stone
paintbrush
paint
glue
paper clips or rubber bands
clear acrylic spray (optional)

1. Find a small, smooth stone to use a paperweight.

2. Invite your child to paint the stone with tempera paint.

3. When the stone has dried, let her glue on a few paper clips or rubber bands for decorations.

4. Later, if you wish, coat the decorated stone with a clear acrylic spray, in an area away from your child.

5. Let her give her Painted Stone Paperweight as a holiday gift.

Holiday Gift~Wrap

You Will Need

newspaper
white tissue paper
tempera paint
eyedroppers or spoons

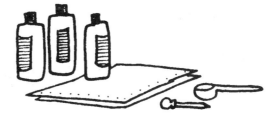

1. Spread newspaper over your work area.

2. Place white tissue paper on top of the newspaper.

3. Set out several colors of tempera paint plus eyedroppers or small spoons.

4. Show your child how to fill an eyedropper or a spoon with paint and then squeeze or dribble drops of the paint over the tissue paper in designs.

5. Encourage him to try making designs in several colors, if he wishes.

6. Allow the tissue paper to dry flat.

7. Use the decorated paper for wrapping Christmas gifts.

One Gift for Christmas

You Will Need

two or more players

1. Sit with your child and her friends in a circle.

2. Start the game by saying, "I am giving a hug for Christmas."

3. Have the next player repeat what you said and add the name of the gift he or she will give; for instance, "I am giving a hug and a candy cane for Christmas."

4. Continue the game in the same manner, offering clues as needed.

5. When the list of gifts becomes too long for the players to remember, choose another child to start a new round of the game.

Hint: For younger children, remembering three or four gifts may be the limit.

Elves' Treasure Hunt

You Will Need

one or more players
treasure
paper
pen

1. Hide a small treasure, such as stickers or colorful pipe cleaners, in the room.

2. On paper, draw a simple map of the room and mark the place where the treasure is hidden with an X.

3. Invite your child and his friends to use the map to find the treasure that Santa has hidden for his elves.

   For More Fun: Let older children hide treasure and draw maps for the other elves to follow.

Toyland

You Will Need

two or more players
glue
pictures of toys
small cards
box

1. Glue pictures of toys onto small cards and place the cards in a box.

2. Have your child and her friends sit in a circle.

3. Let one child begin by choosing a card from the box.

4. Have the child act out how to play with the toy pictured on the card while the other players try to guess what the toy is.

5. Let the first player to guess correctly have the next turn.

6. Continue until everyone has had a chance to play, or as long as interest lasts.

Hop in Santa's Sleigh

You Will Need

three or more players
toy picture cards

1. Give your child and each of his friends one of the toy picture cards from the Toyland game on page 38.

2. Pretend to be Santa driving his sleigh around the room and picking up toys for his trip.

3. As you call out the name of a toy pictured on a card, have the player holding that card "hop aboard" your sleigh by hooking on behind you.

4. Continue until everyone is onboard.

5. When you call out, "Reindeer, up and away!" have all the players tumble to the floor and sit in a circle.

6. Have each player choose a different toy card before you start the game again.

For More Fun: Let older children take turns playing the role of Santa.

What's in Santa's Sack?

You Will Need

three or more players
small toys
pillowcase

1. Have your child and her friends sit in a circle, and place several small toys in the middle.

2. Choose one child to be Santa and give that player a pillowcase to represent Santa's sack.

3. While the other players close their eyes, have "Santa" put one of the toys into the sack.

4. As Santa walks around the circle, invite the other players to feel the outside of the sack and try to guess what toy is inside.

5. Let the first player to guess correctly be Santa for the next round of the game.

6. Continue playing until everyone has had a turn being Santa.

Christmas Bow Toss

You Will Need

two or more players
gift-wrap bows
box
laundry basket or similar container

1. Collect five to ten self-stick gift-wrap bows and place them in a box.

2. Put a laundry basket or a similar container on the floor.

3. Stand with your child and his friends a short distance from the basket and take turns tossing the bows into it.

4. After all the bows have been tossed, count together those that made it into the basket.

5. Choose a new player to start the next round of the game.

For More Fun: Challenge older children by having them take one step backward after each round. How far back can they stand and still get bows into the basket?

Gingerbread

½ cup all-purpose flour
½ cup whole-wheat flour
½ cup wheat germ
2 tsp. baking soda
1½ tsp. ground ginger
1¼ tsp. ground cinnamon
2 egg whites, lightly beaten
1 cup apple-juice concentrate, divided
¼ cup vegetable oil

1. Let your child help you measure the first six ingredients and combine them in a large bowl.

2. Stir in egg whites and ½ cup apple-juice concentrate.

3. Heat remaining ½ cup juice concentrate in a small saucepan.

4. Add warm juice plus vegetable oil to batter and let your child help you stir thoroughly.

5. Pour batter into a greased 8-inch-square baking pan.

6. Bake at 350°F for 35 minutes.

7. Cut into squares when cool.

Elves' Peanut Clusters

1 package chocolate or vanilla pudding
1 cup sugar
½ cup evaporated milk
1 Tbs. butter
1 cup peanuts

1. Let your child help you combine pudding mix, sugar, milk, and butter in a saucepan.

2. Bring the mixture to a boil, stirring constantly.

3. Add peanuts and continue stirring.

4. When the mixture begins to thicken, drop teaspoonfuls of it onto waxed paper.

5. Allow the Elves' Peanut Clusters to cool and harden before serving.

Christmas Grahams

Graham crackers
White creamy frosting
Tube of red icing
Sprinkles (optional)

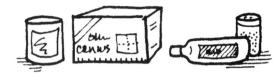

1. Carefully break graham crackers into squares.

2. Set out white creamy frosting and a tube of red icing.

3. Invite your child to spread the white frosting onto the graham cracker squares to represent "tissue-wrapped gifts."

4. Help her squeeze red-icing ribbons and bows onto the squares and add sprinkles, if desired.

5. Serve the Christmas Grahams right away as a snack.

For More Fun: Use food coloring to tint some of the frosting green before spreading it onto the graham crackers.

Crunchy Peanut Butter Balls

½ cup raisins
¼ cup apple-juice concentrate
¼ cup peanut butter
¼ cup powdered milk
1 tsp. vanilla
1 tsp. cinnamon
1 cup nut-like cereal

1. Heat raisins and apple-juice concentrate in a saucepan and boil for about 2 minutes.

2. Pour mixture into a blender container and purée.

3. Combine raisin purée and remaining ingredients in a bowl, adding a few drops of water if mixture is too dry.

4. Let your child help shape the mixture into small balls.

5. Serve right away or refrigerate overnight.

Vanilla Cream "Nog"

2 cups milk
1 tsp. vanilla
1 Tbs. honey
¼ tsp. allspice
½ cup whipping cream

1. Let your child help you combine milk, vanilla, honey, and allspice in a small saucepan.

2. Place over medium heat, stirring frequently to prevent a skin from forming, until just hot but not boiling.

3. Meanwhile, whip cream in a cold glass bowl until stiff peaks form.

4. Pour heated milk into small cups and swirl in the whipped cream.

Red Cranberry Punch

4 cups cranberry drink, chilled
⅛ cup grenadine syrup, chilled
4 cups club soda, chilled
Ice cubes
Strawberry or maraschino cherry halves (optional)

1. In a punch bowl, combine cranberry drink and grenadine syrup.

2. Slowly pour in club soda.

3. Add ice cubes.

4. Garnish with strawberry or maraschino cherry halves, if you wish.